# Passion to Purpose
# Acts of Faith

By
Shemeka Banks

**Copyright © 2021 by Shemeka Banks**

All rights reserved. No part of this publication may be reproduced, distributed, or transmitted in any form or by any means, including photocopying, recording, or other electronic or mechanical methods, without the prior written permission of the publisher, except in the case of brief quotations embodied in critical reviews and certain other non-commercial uses permitted by copyright law.

## Motivational Scriptures

"I consider my life worth nothing to me; my only aim is to finish the race and complete the task the Lord Jesus has given me."

(Acts 20:24 New International Version)

"Now faith is the substance of things hoped for, and the evidence of things not seen."

(Hebrews 11:1 King James Version)

"Looking unto Jesus the author and finisher of our faith; who for the joy that was set before him endured the cross, despising the shame, and is set down at the right hand of the throne of God."

(Hebrews 12:2 King James Version)

# Table of Contents

Introduction Acts of Faith ..... 1
Entering the Faith Zone ..... 9
The Power of Prayer ..... 29
Speaking Spirits ..... 38
Being Intentional ..... 43
Perseverance, Faithfulness, and Consistency ..... 53
Getting Results and Seeing Manifestation ..... 65
Rest and Restore ..... 74
Here's the Challenge: ..... 84
Author Page ..... 93

# Introduction Acts of Faith

Many of us have heard God's still, small voice calling us into our places of destiny. "For I know the plans I have for you," declares the LORD, "plans to prosper you and not to harm you, plans to give you hope and a future" (Jeremiah 29:11 New International Version). When you receive the call of God on your life, whether it is in an HD picture or a little unclear at first, God wants us to trust and obey Him. All you need is a glimpse. Then allow God to show you the way. When he gives you your roadmap to destiny, follow His instructions and obey Him. Doing so will require faith, courage, and commitment to overcome the obstacles you will inevitably face on your journey.

The vision God gives you is the hope that you need to persevere through adversity, doubt, and fear if you keep your eyes focused on Him. It is hope that produces faith. Hebrews 11:1 says, "Now faith is the substance of things hoped for, and the evidence of things not seen." You may see the vision in the spirit of your mind, but it has yet to come to fruition. You get excited seeing the potential that God has on your life, but what will you do with it? It's time to go from just having passion and excitement to manifesting and living out our true purpose in God.

Passion to Purpose, Acts of Faith was written to enlighten, encourage, and empower you to fulfilling your purpose and destiny in God. There is nothing more important than purpose. Without it, life would be empty. Often, we try to go through life seeking happiness in material things and people, but the truth is that happiness and joy are found in God alone. Everything else is temporary without God.

As we discover more of who God is and who He created us to be, we realize that He is very intentional in getting us to the place of destiny that he calls us to be. Everything that you experienced in life so far was part of His plan to draw you closer to Him and to your destiny which is in Him. The closer you get to Him, the closer you get to your destiny which is eternity with Him. That is why it is important to know God and not just chase after material things or stuff with temporary satisfaction but have no God in it. "So we fix our eyes not on what is seen, but on what is unseen, since what is seen is temporary, but what is unseen is eternal." (2 Corinthians 4:18 New International Version)

Our faith is the confidence or trust that we have in God. It leads us to obedience because we know that God has His best in mind for our lives. Our obedience to the will of God for our lives is our actions of faith. It is not enough just to say we believe God. There should be a corresponding action on our part related to God's will and our obedience. That is what we call alignment. The obedience factor can only come into play as we study God's word and hear from Him. You cannot obey what you do not know and cannot hear.

Hearing from God requires intimacy with God. We first must seek Him to get a keener awareness of who God is so that we may know His character and know Him personally for ourselves. Once we have established that relationship with God, then we can obey Him. It is still a choice—a choice to believe what God is saying over everything else. The world may say one thing, but can we still believe God? If we do, our faith will be displayed in our actions by our obedience to Him.

No one starts out walking in the fullness of the call that God has for their life. Even those who have mastered their crafts were once beginners. There may also be some areas where you are walking in obedience and faith, but there are others where you are not so much. That is okay. We must grow and be developed on the journey to becoming everything that God created us to be.

We cannot do this alone. The Holy Spirit is working in and through us ultimately to help us on this journey of fulfilling our purpose in God. The Holy Spirit is our guide. Every experience in our lives is a part of our process. We grow from faith to faith and glory to glory. God intentionally stretches our faith a little further with each experience to develop us into who He has created us to be. Even what we consider our bad experiences, they are working for our good in teaching us lessons. He is not only transforming us into the image of Christ, but He is also maturing us as we become His church, His bride, without a spot or wrinkle.

I remember when I first became a minister in training. I was so excited at first to answer the call of God on my life. I was on fire for God and ready to go. The passion for fulfilling my purpose was so intense, but it wasn't long before my circumstances of that season put that fire out. When I got home, I experienced some issues in my relationship, and not too long after all the excitement, disappointment set in. How was I going to fulfill my purpose while still dealing with domestic issues? How was I going to fulfill my purpose while being halfway in the church and halfway out? I used to put on my best face, but it was not long before I was distracted and off course.

Here I was; God was calling me to this higher level in Him, but I was not ready, or at least I thought I was not. You see, I was too busy focusing on what was not right to see what was. The good news is that God never gave up on me. He may have allowed me to make my own decisions and come to the end of myself and pride, but He certainly did not take His hand off of me. Now, here I am, over ten years later answering the call. Not that everything in my life is perfect now, but I have learned to trust God over what I see. Faith is spiritual fortitude to do what it is that God is calling you to do. It was in the hard times that I learned strength in God. (I prayed a lot.)

God knows the end from the beginning. Nothing we do or experience catches God by surprise. He simply asks for our obedience as He gives the instructions for the journey ahead.

The first set of instructions most of us learn and recognize is His word. The Bible says, "Thy word is a lamp unto my feet, and a light unto my path."

The word or the scriptures is called the 'Logos word of God', and then there is the 'Rhema word,' which is the spoken word of God. The Rhema word is just as important as reading God's written word. However, this can be hard to comprehend when you are just starting your relationship with God. Distinguishing God's voice from any other voice takes time and intimacy.

We have spent a lot of time in the world learning its principles and values. Now our minds will need to be renewed in the word of God to be transformed into who God created us to be fully. We must become studiers and followers of the word to discern the voice of God truly. "My sheep listen to my voice; I know them, and they follow me." (John 10:27 New International Version) "But they will never follow a stranger; in fact, they will run away from him because they do not recognize a stranger's voice." (John 10:5 New International Version)

Starting with God's written word will help uncover many revelations to get you started on the path. Still, as you grow in faith and your intimacy with God, many instructions will be Rhema as you receive the visions and a glimpse of what He has in store for you.

So, here are my questions for you to think about and journal on as we begin this journey from the passion in our hearts to fulfilling God's purpose.

- What is keeping you from answering the call of God on your life?
- Are there some distractions, doubt, or fear?
- What is your most significant obstacle or challenge today?
- Are you aware of your purpose or calling?
- If so, what actions have you taken so far in fulfilling it?
- What further actions does God require of you?

It's easy to say we "have faith" as long as everything is going according to our plans, but what about when we face challenges and obstacles along the way? We must keep in mind that the challenges and obstacles we face are all there to help build our faith and character and not destroy us. Without this part of the process, we would not be ready for the next level of the journey.

It is literally in the tests and trials that we are prepared and developed for our next level in God. You really cannot get ahead of God. He knows what we will do before we do it. He knows what we need before we need it. "2 Consider it pure joy, my brothers and sisters, whenever you face trials of many kinds, 3 because you know that the testing of your faith produces perseverance. 4 Let perseverance finish its work so that you may be mature and complete, not lacking anything." (1 James 2-4 New International Version)

God positions us to be at the right place for destiny to

occur with the right mind, heart, and will to fulfill the purpose He has for us. That is not just positioning, but that is what we call posturing to be at the right place and the right time and be prepared to fulfill purpose while we are there. God makes no mistakes, and indeed, He is not going to start today. He chose you. It is His will. It is your purpose, and no matter what it looks like now, He will see you all the way to fruition. The word says His word will not return unto Him void. God gave you the vision for a reason. Now it is time for you to do your part.

Remember, faith without works is dead. Works meaning action that produces results and the manifestation of the vision God gave you. Now's the time to take what you are so passionate about and seek God as He gives you understanding and clarity and brings the vision to fruition. It will require intentional acts of faith on your part but always remember increase comes from God. No amount of worldly success or achievement can replace an eternity with God. "What profiteth a man to gain the whole world and lose his soul?" (Mark 8:36)

# ENTERING THE FAITH ZONE

It was January 31st, 2021, and my fiancé and I planned a beautiful wedding. This was the day that we would become husband and wife in front of God and all our witnesses. The news was reporting a severe snowstorm. We prayed and hoped that it would not be nearly as bad as predicted. Either way, we woke up the next day to snow on the ground and snow falling out of the sky. You can imagine our disappointment. We both tried hard not to think the worst, but we started getting reports that we may have to cancel, reschedule, or change one of the most important days of our lives. We needed to enter a faith zone. A place where no matter what it looked like, we were going to believe God and stick with God.

We held hands to pray together, and immediately there was a shift in the atmosphere. Then I put on some of our favorite gospel and praise songs, and we sang and danced as if our faith was unshakable. We decided to praise God in advance. Right in the middle of our praise, we received a phone call that the roads were clear and that the wedding can go on. One good report after another, and just about everyone who was supposed to be there, was there. Everything was lovely and what looked like a storm that would have destroyed our plans became the most beautiful beginning of our faith walk together. That's how you start a marriage, and that's how you enter the faith zone!!! God showed us how we could make it through a lifetime together all in one day by praying together, praising together, encouraging one another, and standing in faith together.

One thing that is inevitable on all of our journeys is there will be tests and trials. All sorts of obstacles and challenges will be presented on our journeys that appear greater than us, but they are not greater than our God. It is like David facing Goliath. It looks impossible based on the size or magnitude of the challenge, but it is just an uncircumcised Philistine that we can conquer with one blow if we put our trust in God.

In Matthew, Jesus slept through a storm while everyone else on the ship panicked. Matthew 8:26 says He replied, "You of little faith, why are you so afraid?" Then He got up and rebuked the winds and the waves, and it was completely calm. Everyone on that boat had the power to defeat the enemy (fear) and enter the rest of God, but they did not have the faith to do it. That is why they woke Jesus. Jesus responded by calming the storm but also letting them know that they, too, could have spoken to the storm and it would have obeyed, but because of their lack of faith, they woke Him up to do it.

Quick question: What are you waiting on God to do in your life that He already gave you the power to do?

Then there are also battles. There is no victory where there is no challenge. No matter how great the battle may seem, remember, God is greater. To face spiritual warfare, we must have on the whole armor of God. The armor is how we spiritually prepare for the attacks of the enemy. There is an enemy who does not want to see God's will done in your life. The enemy doesn't want you living victoriously or even knowing that you have the power and the ability to win over all the forces of evil! Not only that but also to live a life of power and authority.

"I will give you the keys of the kingdom of heaven. Whatever you bind on earth will be bound in heaven, and whatever you loose on earth will be loosed in heaven." (Matthew 18:18 New International Version)

It was God's will in the first place that we have the power over Satan. Yes, he will attack, that is just what he does, but he has been stripped of his power by Jesus. That was God's plan from the very beginning of the fall of mankind. "I will put enmity between you and the woman, and between your offspring and hers; he will crush your head, and you will strike his heel." (Genesis 3:15 New International Version).

Although we already have the victory in Jesus, it doesn't mean that there won't be spiritual warfare. 2 Corinthians 10:4-5 says, "The weapons we fight with are not the weapons of the world. On the contrary, they have divine power to demolish strongholds. We demolish arguments and every pretension that sets itself up against the knowledge of God, and we take captive every thought to make it obedient to

Christ." We know that the enemy will attack you in any way possible, but we have weapons from God. You can overcome your fears and obstacles to pursue a life of purpose in God. Yes, Satan will attack, but we are overcomers, and in the end, we win!!!

The Bible says, "Therefore put on the full armor of God, so that when the day of evil comes, you may be able to stand your ground, and after you have done everything, to stand. 14 Stand firm then, with the belt of truth buckled around your waist, with the breastplate of righteousness in place,15 and with your feet fitted with the readiness that comes from the gospel of peace.16 In addition to all this, take up the shield of faith, with which you can extinguish all the flaming arrows of the evil one.17 Take the helmet of salvation and the sword of the Spirit, which is the word of God. 18 And pray in the Spirit on all occasions with all kinds of prayers and requests. With this in mind, be alert and always keep on praying for all the Lord's people." (Ephesians 6:13-18 New International Version)

There is more to it than just showing up ready to answer the call of God for your life. But know, the moment we do, there will be challenges, storms, and battles but don't get discouraged. Have faith and let the Lord will fight for you. This is how we live victoriously, by faith in God.

Even still, having experienced tests and trials, it is not a time to quit and give up on God. Instead, this is when we must stand in faith, go forward in faith, and overcome by faith. How do we get to this place of victory? I call it the faith zone. It is a place where we know, without a shadow of a doubt, that God has chosen us, equipped us, prepared us, is protecting us on this journey, so we are not afraid to face the challenges and obstacles in our lives and live out our God-given purposes and destinies.

God already knows what we are going to face before we face it. The challenge was not intended to take you out but rather to help you grow in your faith and relationship with Him. This way, you are fully developed and prepared for what is to come. There is a saying, "For every level, there's a new devil.". Satan operates from our fear, but when we determine that we will trust God no matter what, his tactics no longer work. Remember, he has been stripped of his power.

## The Path

"Thy word is a lamp unto my feet, and a light unto my path." (Psalm 119:105 King James Version)

The lamp unto my feet is essential because it helps me see where I am currently. What is my current mindset, habits, actions, and position? The light unto my path is also essential because it helps me see where God is taking me. It gives me encouragement, hope, a vision, instructions, a map, etc. It's all about being in the right place of destiny to fulfill God's purpose in our lives. I may not be there yet, but I will get there if I stay on the path.

The path is spiritual. Remember, we are in the world but not of it. So, to fully understand this, you must know that while we are in the flesh here on earth, we are spiritual beings on a spiritual journey that manifests itself in the natural world. "By faith we understand that the universe was formed at God's command, so that what is seen was not made out of what was visible." (Hebrews 11:3 New International Version)

There is a path that is specially designed for you. Even though there will be opposition and challenges, you may not even feel qualified to answer the call of God that is on your life but trust God anyhow. It is His plan, not ours. We are just active participates or willing vessels.

God draws us closer to Him as we continue to grow in faith on our journeys. Believe God over your insecurities or intellect. He will shock you with evidence. Faith is the evidence of things not seen. You don't see it yet. That is why it requires faith, but when it manifests by faith, you will know and testify that it was God. If you could do it in your ability, you wouldn't need God, and it wouldn't require faith.

When we have faith in God despite obstacles and challenges, it unlocks the supernatural power of God that reveals the manifestation of God's will for our lives and His unfailing love. In this constant relationship and intimacy with Him, we learn of His will for our lives and learn to trust Him in it.

God has a plan, but we must do our part and submit to His plan. The world has its way, and God has His. Romans 12:2

(New King James Version) says, "Do not conform to the pattern of this world but be transformed by the renewing of your mind. Then you will be able to test and approve what God's will is— his good, pleasing and perfect will."

Another great scripture to keep in mind is John 16:33 (New International Version), and it says, "I have told you these things, so that in me you may have peace. In this world, you will have trouble. But take heart! I have overcome the world." This scripture reassures us that we can be confident that we will overcome and have peace as we go on our journey.

Another scripture that comes to mind related to the path is Matthew 7:13-14. 13 (New International Version) "Enter through the narrow gate. For wide is the gate, and broad is the road that leads to destruction, and many enter through it. 14 But small is the gate and narrow the road that leads to life, and only a few find it."

The world can be so confusing because of the amount of noise. There are so many thoughts and ideas suggested to us. There is a path that goes beyond this world, and the only way to find it is in the spiritual from intimacy with God. This intimacy will open our spiritual hears and eyes. God will speak to us and show us things to help us along the way to fulfill the purpose he has for our lives.

When David faced Goliath, he relied solely on God to give him the victory. Ultimately it was part of his purpose. In previous battles, David's intimacy with God built his faith to face a giant that everyone was afraid of. He knew the same God who protected him and gave him the victory would do it again, and so David was ready to face the giant because God prepared him.

One thing to keep in mind is that God never puts more on us than we can bear and that He is with us every step of the way. Not only was David going to face a giant at that time, but he was also anointed as King for later in his journey. Every part of the process has a purpose. "The Lord who rescued me from the paw of the lion and the paw of the bear will rescue me from the hand of this Philistine." Saul said to David, "Go, and the LORD be with you." (1 Samuel 17:37 New International Version)

David was a shepherd boy, but God had a plan for David and his life beyond being a shepherd boy. However, being a shepherd boy was part of his preparation. Don't despise humble beginnings. Each level we experience on this journey is intentional. God is intentional, and as we face challenges, our faith grows exponentially. That means we will have to face a few obstacles with God on our side to see that He is more than able to bring us through to victory. Once you know that you become like David, and you are not afraid of the giant; instead, you are talking to the giants in your life and reminding them who really has the power. Power belongs to God, in which he gave us the keys.

David wrote Psalm 23, and it demonstrates the level of intimacy he had with God. This is the kind of relationship God wants us to have with Him on our path. I read and recite this scripture quite often as a reminder that God is with me on this journey. We are not alone, and therefore we do not have to fight alone.

Psalm 23 (King James Version)

"1 The Lord is my shepherd; I shall not want. 2 He maketh me to lie down in green pastures: he leadeth me beside the still waters. 3 He restoreth my soul: he leadeth me in the paths of righteousness for his name's sake. 4 Yea, though I walk through the valley of the shadow of death, I will fear no evil: for thou art with me; thy rod and thy staff they comfort me. 5 Thou preparest a table before me in the presence of mine enemies: thou anointest my head with oil; my cup runneth over. 6 Surely goodness and mercy shall follow me all the days of my life: and I will dwell in the house of the Lord forever."

**Fulfilling Purpose**

One thing about God that is so amazing and awesome is that when He created mankind, He did not leave us here wondering what we should do and how we should do it. He gave His instructions from the very beginning to be fruitful and multiply. That is our original purpose from God. Therefore, the parable of the talents is so important and relevant to our lives.

God wants to see a return on His investment. What has God placed inside of you? What gift, passion, talent, or vision has He given you? Cultivate it and make it fruitful for the advancement of the kingdom. The more you operate in your purpose with the Holy Spirit leading you, the more you will win over souls for Christ. That is what you call winning exponentially!!!

This is a faith walk. You will need to have faith to fulfill your purpose. If you are not sure what your purpose is, ask God to help you on this journey in ways you can bring glory to Him. He has given us all gifts. He wants to use the gifts He gave us to fulfill our purpose. We are all uniquely made, and all our lives are different, but we all have something we can do to bring God glory. I'll tell you a straightforward way, and that is through your testimony. Share what God has done for you, and that is how we give him glory. Now we may all do it in different ways. Some will do it through songs, some will do it through art, some will do it through speech, some will do it through books, some will do it through movies and plays. The possibilities are truly endless with God. New ideas are being created every day.

Whatever gift God gave you, that is what you use. Some say do something you love, and you will never work a day in your life. Others say, do what you are strong and gifted at, and it will come naturally to you. I believe we should do both. What we love to do and what we are gifted in, God can use us with both. The real key is asking God what He would like for you to do and do that.

If God gave you a gift, He wants you to use that gift to glorify Him. When we are passionate about something or someone, our hearts are in it, so we tend to give it our all. We also can find joy in what we do when we are passionate about it. It can be one of the most fulfilling experiences, living out our purpose.

Also, keep in mind that when we first gave our lives to God, we were so passionate about the things of God. We were ready to share our testimony with anyone with who we came in contact. We were ready to follow His word and obey Him. We were ready to fulfill His purpose on earth by any means necessary. But somewhere along the journey, that passion started to dwindle as we face daily challenges, even as a believer. What God wants us to do is to continue to draw closer to Him because as we are more intimate with Him, He reignites that passion inside of us, via the Holy Spirit, as fuel to our flames. God knows how to get us back in alignment.

Romans 2:4 says, "Or do you show contempt for the riches of his kindness, forbearance, and patience, not realizing that God's kindness is intended to lead you to repentance?" God knows exactly want we need on our paths to purpose. He is always drawing us to Him but are we taking the time out of our so-called busy schedules to seek Him? Or is it our ambitions in worldly affairs that hinder our focus on Him and extinguishes our flame for the things of God? If so, God knows how to draw us back to Him and His heart. You know the old saying, you can catch more bees with honey than vinegar. Apparently, it is true because instead of killing us while we are off track for our disloyalty and disobedience, he draws us back in with His goodness and kindness. Isn't that sweet?

Besides, the world has nothing to offer us except temporary satisfactions, but true fulfillment is in God. We must first know who we are in God to understand our identity in God. We are His creation, but also, we are His children. Our purpose is directly associated with our identity. If you do not know who you are or why you are here, you are bound to let just about anyone dictate your life. That is why so many people are under the enemy's control, but when we know who we are in God, our relationship and view of God changes.

Because of the enemy's lies and deception, many people are not operating in their true gifts and talents either because society told them they are not good enough or even capable. Still, where we lack ability, God is able to do exceedingly and abundantly more than we can ever ask or think. It will require faith in God to do that thing that you know in your heart that you were called and created to do.

If you have spent your whole life being trained to think a particular way, it will require a paradigm shift to see things

God's way. If you feel called or know you are called to do something, it can be hard to change your limiting beliefs and do it. Limiting beliefs are those beliefs that we have picked up over time from different sources (our frame of reference) that hold us back from our full potential.

Limiting beliefs are just what they are called, beliefs that limit us. For some, it could be their belief towards the opposite sex that keeps them from having the desired relationship that God intended for them to have. For some, it may be the beliefs they have towards money that keep them in a poverty mindset and lacking resources. It may also be in their ability to see a vision come to fruition, so they quit before they even get started.

I can give many examples because it is simply what you believe based on what you have been taught or experienced. You can, however, retrain your brain in those areas and seek a revelation from God. It won't be easy to shift your thinking if it is deeply rooted in your heart and mind, but it is possible. One thing that works for me is reciting God's word on the matter and intimate prayer with God. I like to remind myself what God said in His word.

Even still, no matter how challenging it is to change, when we know that God is calling for a change in our lives, we must give up our old way of thinking and surrender to His will. Easier said than done. I know. That is why we have to stay in the word and pray to learn to trust God no matter the situation or circumstance. We must renew our minds in the word daily.

That is the only way to shift to this new mindset of faith in God. Otherwise, you will continue to repeat the same actions. They call it insanity to keep repeating the same actions and expecting a different result. If you always do what you have always done, you will always get the result you always have. To see or get something different, we must do something different, which starts with our thoughts. Actions are a result of what we think or believe concerning a matter. Therefore, we must change our mindset to change our actions.

Do not worry about rejection. You can change and decide to live a life of purpose and destiny in God without anyone else's permission. The Bible says a prophet is not a prophet in his own home. Why is that? Why can't a prophet be a prophet in his family and community? Well, because being a prophet is not the popular culture in most families and communities. Do not believe me? Go around for a day and tell everyone you are a prophet and watch their responses. Most will just say, yeah, right. Especially those closest to you. No, but really.

What if you are a prophet, but you are not operating in that gift because it is not popular culture? We all have access to the prophetic through the Holy Spirit. Another reason you may not get embraced with open arms is that your family and friends know the old you. They cannot imagine that this person who was once one way and is now another. It just does not make any sense. It is hard to change people's opinions about you. Here is my tip for that. Do not. Focus on God and not people because people will have you all messed up in the head related to your identity and purpose. Many people don't know their own identity and purpose to be trying to tear yours into pieces. If you live for their acceptance, then you will die from their rejection.

I am saying all this because you are becoming who you were designed to be. Other people may not see it. They may disagree with you. They may have seen you struggle and cannot see how it is even possible. Listen to me. Do it anyway. A meme floating around says, "when God called you, it wasn't a conference call." So why wait for everyone around you to agree when they didn't get the memo. Agree with God in faith, and by faith, and you will see the manifestation. That alone will speak for itself.

Fulfilling purpose would not require faith if there were no opposition. This life is all about faith in God. The enemy knows that if you ever get a glimpse of who you really are and what you are called to do, you would be unstoppable. You would know your worth, identity, and purpose and act on it. I challenge you today to ask God in what areas He requires you to change your mindset and actions by faith. Then apply the principles I am going to share with you in this book. If you are already applying them, great! Ask God to reveal some other areas where you are not so much. We are all always learning and growing. I like how Paul put it. If we are humble, then this should go without saying:

12 Not that I have already obtained all this, or have already arrived at my goal, but I press on to take hold of that for which Christ Jesus took hold of me. 13 Brothers and sisters, I do not consider myself yet to have taken hold of it. But one thing I do: Forgetting what is behind and straining toward what is ahead,

14 I press on toward the goal to win the prize for which God has called me heavenward in Christ Jesus. (Philippians 3:12-16 New International Version)

Satan does not like the idea of us glorifying God in this capacity because it can affect others. When we have the victory and share our testimonies, other people are encouraged to trust God and get the victory in their lives too. That is why he has been up against you your whole life. I know you tried to do it Mama's way or Daddy's way, but it just did not work for you. So, you tried it your way, and it failed. You may have even tried to take the easy route but come to find there is no such thing.

Step out in faith. Nothing is going to change until you do. Stop talking yourself out of your destiny in God and a much more victorious lifestyle across the board. Not in just one area of your life but all areas of your life. That is how God works. It may seem impossible from where you stand today but know that God gets more glory when we face challenges that seem impossible and conquer them by faith in Him. Those are the most incredible testimonies.

Always pray because God can do what you cannot do. And remember, He created you, so He is for you. He wants you to be successful because when you are, it gives Him glory. Let your excuses and fears motivate you instead of disabling you to take the first steps by faith, and eventually, you will get there if you do not give up. Some say to take the lemons from life (those bad experiences) and make some lemonade. What God has for you will blow your mind. Don't get too caught up with where you may be in any area of your life right now. God does miracles. The greater the challenge, the more the glory!!!

There is a scripture about God giving a group of people talents. I am sure you may have heard it before. In the story, you will see how each person responds differently to God's gift of talents. We are stewards of the blessings God has given us, including our gifts and talents. Did you know your talent is a resource? The Bible says your gift will make room for you. Be mindful that a talent was worth about twenty years of labor. Do the math and put it together; however, God gives it to you. Seek Him for the revelation. This is a scripture I read for accountability. One day, He will hold us accountable for what we did and did not do.

## The Parable of the Talents

Matthew 25:14-30 (English Standard Version)

14 "For it will be like a man going on a journey, who called his servants and entrusted to them his property. 15 To one, he gave five talents, to another two, to another one, to each according to his ability. Then he went away. 16 He who had received the five talents went at once and traded with them, and he made five talents more. 17 So also, he who had the two talents made two talents more. 18 But he who had received the one talent went and dug in the ground and hid his master's money. 19 Now, after a long time, the master of

those servants came and settled accounts with them. 20 And he who had received the five talents came forward, bringing five talents more, saying, 'Master, you delivered to me five talents; here, I have made five talents more.' 21 His master said to him, 'Well done, good and faithful servant. You have been faithful over a little; I will set you over much. Enter the joy of your master.' 22 And he also who had the two talents came forward, saying, 'Master, you delivered to me two talents; here, I have made two talents more.' 23 His master said to him, 'Well done, good and faithful servant. You have been faithful over a little; I will set you over much. Enter the joy of your master.' 24 He also who had received the one talent came forward, saying, 'Master, I knew you to be a hard man, reaping where you did not sow, and gathering where you scattered no seed, 25 so I was afraid, and I went and hid your talent in the ground. Here, you have what is yours.' 26 But his master answered him, 'You wicked and slothful servant! You knew that I reap where I have not sown and gather where I scattered no seed? 27 Then you ought to have invested my money with the bankers, and at my coming, I should have received what was my own with interest. 28 So take the talent from him and give it to him who has the ten talents. 29 For to everyone who has will more be given, and he will have an abundance. But from the one who has not, even what he has will be taken away. 30 And cast the worthless servant into the outer darkness. In that place, there will be weeping and gnashing of teeth.'"

God will not force you to fulfill your purpose and answer the call of God on your life. You have free will. Here is my advice: ask God what He wants you to do with your life and step out in faith and do it. He will give you the gifts and talents, spiritually and naturally. He will give you the vision. He will ignite the passion inside of you to be your fuel. He will see you through, but you will equally have to obey Him, seek Him and do your part.

This book will focus on three crucial principles regarding acts of faith that help us on our journey of purpose. These principles are the power of prayer, speaking spirits, and being intentional. As you go on this journey, I want you to try God at His word and keep track of the victories you see happening in your life as a result. Remember, there will be obstacles and storms, but the storm always comes before the calm.

# The Power of Prayer

God gave us prayer as a form of communication with Him. Although many of us are taught how to pray by religion starting out, there is another level of prayer. It is when we speak to God sincerely and purposefully. We come to God with our whole heart, not just with rhetoric and religious dogma. We also wait to hear Him speak back. Jeremiah 29:13 (New International Version) says, "You will seek me and find me when you seek me with all your heart." This is the beginning of intimacy with God, prayer from your heart to His.

Many of us came to God in a broken place. A place where we knew that we needed Him and that if He did not step in, we simply would not make it. God then steps in and comforts us and reassures us that no challenge or obstacle is too big for Him. He is the creator of everything. We must get to this state of brokenness because, otherwise, we would rely on our strength, wisdom, and earthly possessions and convince ourselves that we do not need God. When we become so self-sufficient, people even go so far as to say that there is no God at all, but Psalm 14:1 says (King James Version), "The fool hath said in his heart is no God. They are corrupt, they have done abominable works, there is none that doeth good."

When we pray, we acknowledge God, and He hears us and responds to our prayers. We also acknowledge our need for supernatural intervention of some form. Prayer is an act of faith because to pray, and I mean genuinely pray, not just recite words that have no meaning to you whatsoever, you must believe that God is real and that He hears you and that He will answer your prayer. The reason why praying is considered faith because we believe in God and God is a Spirit, so we do not see Him in the natural. Therefore, we must have faith in order to believe in the power of prayer.

One of the most famous prayers and the model prayer that Jesus used to teach us how to pray is Matthew 6:9-13 (King James Version). "9 After this manner therefore pray ye: Our Father which art in heaven, Hallowed be thy name. 10 Thy kingdom come, thy will be done in earth, as it is in heaven. 11 Give us this day our daily bread. 12 And forgive us our debts, as we forgive our debtors. 13 And lead us not into temptation, but deliver us from evil: For thine is the kingdom, and the power, and the glory, forever. Amen."

Growing up, I was taught to say this prayer, but it was not until later in life that I learned what it meant. When we pray, we need to know and understand what we are saying. It is not enough just to quote scripture if it is not in our hearts. I know that my parents were teaching me the foundation and doing their part to train me. I am not saying that this is not a great place to start. I am saying that until we understand and are praying from our heart to God, then it is just words and not true intimacy with God.

Everyone knows the good, old, faithful prayer, God is great, and God is good. It was such a simple prayer to say as a child that it did make sense when we said the words right. That was the problem half the time. We were not saying the words right, or maybe it is different versions of this prayer. The good thing is that, as a child, I understood. Another famous prayer that I recited as a child was "Now Thy Lay Me." This prayer was also simple to understand, although a deeper revelation of "I pray the Lord my soul to take" did not come immediately. I just knew that if anything was going to happen to me while I was asleep, like a monster under the bed eating me up, I wanted God to take me with Him.

The Bible says to train up a child how they should go to not depart from them when they get old. As parents, the training we do, whether our children obey or rebel, is vital because they will understand in time as they mature. We should train them on how to pray and study God's word. We should also be an example of obeying God's word. No, we will not always get it right, but we also should protect their innocence as we raise them to begin their journey.

Like David, they may be kids now, but one day they will grow up, and when they do, God has a plan for their life. Also, like David, it does not begin when they become adults. God's plan for their lives is activated the moment they are born. It is our responsibility to train them. Most of the time, you cannot give what you do not have, and you cannot teach what you do not know. That still does not stop God's plan for them. They, too, will have the opportunity to come to Christ.

I say this because if you are like me, you learned about prayer as a child, and you may have quoted all kinds of scriptures, but there was a point when it went beyond just quoting and became a part of your heart. It was at the moment when it started to mean something deeper to you, and, suddenly, you began to say prayers that you never heard before. You began to talk to God and tell Him what you wanted, and eventually, the prayers got a little deeper from wants and needs to praise and thank Him for what He has already done.

God wants us to communicate with Him always. "Rejoice always, pray without ceasing, give thanks in all circumstances; for this is the will of God in Christ Jesus for you." (1 Thessalonians 5:16-18 King James Version). He wants to hear our wants and needs. He also loves when we praise Him. This is the type of reliance He wants us to have with Him. This is the type of trust He wants us to have in Him.

Proverbs 3:5-6 says (King James Version), "5 Trust in the Lord with all thine heart; and lean not unto thine own understanding.6 In all thy ways acknowledge him, and he shall direct thy paths." Let us face it; we need Him on this journey called life. There is no life without Him. We are just lost sheep without Him. We are wandering through life, just trying to survive and make the most of it.

Oh, but when you give your life to God, it is a brand-new life. You see things you have never seen before. You experience things you never experienced before. You learn things you have never known before. It is almost as if you never really lived until that moment. God begins to show you His will and purpose for your life, and as we grow closer to Him, we begin to see His purpose manifested in us and through us.

It is a whole different lifestyle. We are in the world but not of it. Our perspective and view have changed, and now we are beginning to see things spiritually and not carnally. Being in this world does not come without its challenges, and prayer allows us to talk to God all about it. Philippians 4:6 says, "6 Be careful for nothing; but in everything by prayer and supplication with thanksgiving let your requests be made known unto God." I love how Paul says 'with thanksgiving' because it is a blessing to have this privilege to talk to God the way we do and have Him answer our prayers the way He does. It is not because we are perfect people but because He loves us. Knowing how much God cares for us can bring us so much joy when we pray.

In the Old Testament, the people during those times prayed also, but if they disobeyed God or sinned, they would have to sacrifice to God for the atonement of their sins. This determined whether they were in right standing with God and if they could receive blessings from God. We go to God openly and boldly now because of the finished work of Christ. It is Christ's blood that gave atonement for our sins once and for all. With that being said, we can go openly to God in prayer with whatever request that we may have. The ultimate sacrifice has already been given, thus giving us access.

**Ask, Believe, Receive.**

John 16:23-24 says, "23In that day you will no longer ask me anything. Very truly, I tell you, my Father will give you whatever you ask in my name. 24Until now, you have not asked for anything in my name. Ask, and you will receive, and your joy will be complete." When we pray to God in Jesus' name, we receive what we pray for. This is all because Jesus paid the ultimate price for our sins. It is through Him that we can have a restored relationship with the Father despite our sinful nature. The blood covers us. Jesus intercedes for us as the precious lamb of God. "For God so loved the world that he gave his only begotten son that whosoever believeth in him shall not perish but shall have everlasting life." (John 3:16 King James Version)

"21 Jesus replied, "Truly I tell you, if you have faith and do not doubt, not only can you do what was done to the fig tree, but also you can say to this mountain, 'Go, throw yourself into the sea,' and it will be done. 22 If you believe, you will receive whatever you ask for in prayer." (Matthew 21:21-22 New International Version). God wants us to have the kind of faith to move mountains, but it starts with prayer. We must ask God in Jesus' name and believe that God will do it and receive whatever you asked God for because of His son Jesus.

Now I am not talking about asking God for random things that we want to glorify our flesh, but rather, if it is in His will, He will do it. His word is His will, so it is not meant to suit our flesh but rather to please God and fulfill His purpose. If it is in His word as truth, then that makes it qualifiable. But if it is solely to please our flesh and disobey God, it is a waste of breath even asking because God will not lie, and His word will not return unto Him void. "So shall my word be that goes out from my mouth; it shall not return to me empty, but it shall accomplish that which I purpose, and shall succeed in the thing for which I sent it." (Isaiah 55:11 New International Version)

The world constantly tries to distort God's word and uses it for earthly advantages. Prayer is a principle and law that works for the godly and the ungodly. However, just because someone is praying does not mean they pray to the same true and living God. Just because someone has something does not mean it came from God. Like Elijah, when he challenged all of Jezebel's prophets, they called on their god, Baal, and Elijah called on the one true and living God. They spent all day calling on their god, and nothing happened, but Elijah upped the ante and made the challenge even more, and God showed up and made His presence known.

Jezebel's god was Baal, and that is who she worshipped, and her whole kingdom worshiped Baal, but they still appeared to be blessed, although the false god they worshiped had no power. It is possible to gain earthly power, position, and possessions and lose your soul. God does not want us to worship idols. He is a jealous God. He wants us to trust Him only. When we pray to God, He listens.

While we are on this journey, we must study God's word to know His will, so as we face opposition and trials, we know how to pray and what to pray for. If it is in His will, finances, provisions, healing, restoration, forgiveness, purpose, our needs met, visions and prophecies, guidance, and the list goes on and on – it belongs to the believer.

# SPEAKING SPIRITS

When God created the world, He used words, and since we are made in God's likeness and image, we also have that same power. It is an act of faith because it is more than just saying words or affirmations. Affirmations do not work if you do not believe what you are saying in your heart. The Bible says, out of the mouth, the heart speaks. Therefore, it is an act of faith because we speak in agreement with what is in our hearts, and in order to draw it out or bring it to fruition, we have to speak it.

## What is in our hearts?

What do we genuinely believe? To tap into the power of words, we must become intentional with the words we use and, ultimately, how we think. Not only in how we think but what we meditate on. We do not control every thought that is suggested, but we do, however, decide what we meditate on. Meditation leads to penetration of not just the conscious mind but our hearts. That is also why it is vital to meditate on the word because it becomes our beliefs and eventually our words and actions.

I shall have what I decree. God created the whole world using just His words. We were made in His image, so in the simplest terms I can think of, we too have the power to speak things into existence. Why you may ask, do I not have the brand-new Porsche I claimed in 2005? The only thing I would say to that is, did you speak it with all conviction? Meaning, did you say what you said also believing it, or did you say it with no expectation or intention of doing anything at all to obtain it? I think this is where some people miss it. They think by wishing for a Porsche, that is all that they need to do, but I disagree. If you want a harvest, you have to plant a seed. That is an action. Speaking is also an action but keep in mind the Holy Spirit will give you further instructions when needed.

Another thing to keep in mind is that in the tongue lies the power of life and death. "Death and life are in the power of the tongue: and they that love it shall eat the fruit thereof." (Proverbs 18:2) When we speak, we should be speaking life and existence for that which we are believing. We are creators just like God and just how He formed the world with words; our words have the power to manifest in the natural as well.

"Truly, I say to you, whoever says to this mountain, 'Be taken up and thrown into the sea,' and does not doubt in his heart, but believes that what he says will come to pass, it will be done for him." (Mark 11:23 English Standard Version) When we have faith and speak, we will see what we say come to pass in some shape, form, or fashion. I will put it like this: we should speak what we seek until we see what we say. If you do not want it to come to fruition, then simply do not say it. We will eat the fruit of our lips. If it is bitter and not sweet, we should go back to the source, our thoughts.

Were they spoken at a time when you were bitter, angry, stressed, or sad? We must watch our words while feeling down because we do not want bitterness multiplying in our lives. Instead of speaking in anger or revenge, we must be intentional and recognize the power of words and communicate what we want and not what we do not.

Out of the mouth, the heart speaks. The only way to shift our current circumstances is to get at the root of our words. If words come from the heart, then words are based on what we believe. When we speak or do anything that is not true to our beliefs, it is like our heart says, not so, and it is dead because belief or faith as it relates to what I am describing in this book only produces fruit only when it is genuine. You cannot trick the spirit realm, but you can change what you believe.

It is not easy to change your deeply rooted beliefs no matter how much they do not serve you. Our beliefs are thoughts and ideas that have taken root and produce fruit in our lives. To change a belief, the source of the belief must be uprooted entirely. We should challenge the way we think by the source. Is it from God and in His word, or is it from popular culture? After we check our beliefs, it is essential to uproot and change what needs to be changed. If you do not like the fruit, get rid of the root.

Let's speak on the type of fruit the Holy Spirit will produce when operating in us and through us. We are in alignment instead of the flesh, determine what is good or not. God determines what is good or evil. He clarifies when He gives us the fruit of the spirit: love, joy, peace, forbearance, kindness, goodness, faithfulness, gentleness, and self-control.

He then clarifies the works of the flesh: idolatry, witchcraft, hatred, variance, emulations, wrath, strife, seditions, heresies, envy, murders, drunkenness, reveling, and the like.

When we take account of our actions and fruit, we can see where it all stems from. If it is the flesh, uproot it by starving it. If it is the Spirit of God, then we know we are in God's will because He is living inside us, and the word says we shall know each other by our fruit. Before we judge other people, we should start with ourselves, self-evaluate our own fruit, and make the necessary changes.

If you want to frame your life with your words, you will want to start there with your thoughts and beliefs. I am a Christian. I believe in Christ. Repeatedly in my life, I have seen the fruit of my faith in God. So, there is no doubt in my life when my beliefs are lined up with scripture. When I allow my flesh to take the lead, then I see the fruit of the flesh, which is death.

Galatians 6:7-9 King James Version

"7 Be not deceived; God is not mocked: for whatsoever a man soweth, that shall he also reap. 8 For he that soweth to his flesh shall of the flesh reap corruption; but he that soweth to the Spirit shall of the Spirit reap life everlasting."

Going back to how life and death are in the power of the tongue, faith is a seed. Our beliefs are seeds. When we speak to them, they will either produce life or death. That is how powerful our words are. People have even seen this work even in the natural. They have done studies of people who spoke to the plants or sung to their plants and saw enormous healthier growth.

"15 See, I set before you today life and prosperity, death and destruction. 16 For I command you today to love the Lord your God, to walk in obedience to Him, and to keep His commands, decrees and laws; then you will live and increase, and the Lord your God will bless you in the land you are entering to possess." (Deuteronomy 30:15-16 New International Version)

If you want prosperity, speak in alignment with wealth. If you want good health, speak in alignment with good health. If you want anything in God's will, you must speak it. It is the foundation for which the whole earth was formed. Speak over your life. Affirm God's word in your life on purpose and see how it shapes and changes your circumstances and reality.

## BEING INTENTIONAL

We must watch our thoughts because they become our words and our words become our actions. Watch your actions because they become your habits. Our habits become our character, and our character becomes our destiny. That means be careful what you think because it will determine your words, actions, patterns, character, and, ultimately, your future. Being intentional with your thoughts and words will make a world of difference in your life but let us go a little bit further.

Being intentional is an act of faith because faith without works is dead. Our actions display what we genuinely believe. A simple illustration I learned as a child was faith is just as simple as sitting on a chair. We believe the chair will hold us up, so without a second thought, we sit down. We rarely question the chair unless there is something wrong. So, we act by what we believe.

When we are intentional, our actions line up with God's word. God already gave us the solution and answers in His word, but we still, for whatever reason, try to do it our own way. Having a vision is a godly principle that we should not ignore. However, once we have the vision and take consistent, intentional action, we will see results. Purpose and vision go hand in hand. When God gives us a glimpse into our future, we can see ourselves overcoming obstacles and operating in God's will. It is His purpose for us, but we must go through the process in order to see destiny fulfilled.

What do you do with the vision? You write the vision and make it plain. You materialize it or manifest it by your faith in God and your actions.

"Where there is no vision, the people perish." Proverbs 29:18 (King James Version) The visions God gives us are seeds. They fuel us for purposeful and intentional living. When we do not have a vision, we get caught up in mindless activity and find ourselves spiritually dead. We do not have the fuel even to get up some mornings because there is nothing to live for. Material things only give temporary satisfaction. They do not give us the passion for having true lasting happiness and joy. It is only when we have a purposeful vision that we are moved to keep going forward.

If you want to change that, ask God for a vision. You may find yourself creating visions for yourself. Close your eyes for a good five minutes each morning and intentionally see the life that you want. Do not criticize or talk yourself out of it but pray and then take intentional actions to manifest. Life is so much more fulfilling when we realize the power God placed inside of every one of us.

## Plan

It is no wonder there are no results. You have not planned anything. There is an old saying that says, "When you fail to plan, you plan to fail." One of the most critical parts of any goal or vision is planning. Write the vision and make it plain but also be sure to develop an action plan. No one starts off the journey already knowing everything, but we know what we need to know to get started. We need God to order our steps and then execute as lead by the Spirit.

## Godly Character

We inevitably pick up habits from our environments in the world. Let's be clear God has a standard, and we must be careful to make sure that our lives line up with the word of God. It is easy to pick up on cussing and smoking when you are around it consistently. We must be intentional about our dealings, engagements, environments, and even people we surround ourselves with. Sometimes the decluttering that needs to be done is not stuff but the unhealthy relationships, toxic places, and activities that do not please God. Because habits that do not glorify God can be what is holding us back, it would be a shame if the only thing holding you back is your decisions. When you know better, you will do better.

We all have decisions to make regarding our destiny. Yes, God is forgiving. Yes, He is loving. Yes, He is a restorer but let us be honest, too. Do we take advantage of grace? The answer is yes. No matter what you try to do in life, it means nothing if it was not in the will of God. The word says only what we do for God will last. In the end, that is all that matters. Not what kind of car you drove, what kind of house you bought, what kind of clothing you wore. God wants your heart, not your facade. It less about what we see on the outside and more about what we see on the inside.

The word of God is the most powerful tool we have. It has story after story of successes and failures. If we do our part in the matter, we will see God's results manifested in our lives daily. Sometimes obeying God is the biggest challenge. Why? Well, Paul puts it best. It is our flesh. Our flesh is enmity with God, and it does not seek to please God but rather itself.

Obeying God has its rewards. God says He is the rewarder of those who diligently seek Him. He also says, "Seek ye first the kingdom, and all of its righteousness and all these things will be added unto you." (Matthew 6:13 King James Version) It also says, "Delight thyself in the LORD, and he shall give thee the desires of thine heart." (Psalms 37:4 King James Version) There is scripture after scripture of God's promises to us. There are also scriptures about the price of sin. It consistently says the wages of sin are death but somehow, we fool ourselves into believing that we got over.

No, the death may not be physical but instead spiritual. So, you may not even notice that you are spiritually dead. Just take a moment and see how far off track you have gotten with fulfilling purpose, manifesting the vision, working on being a better steward, giving, and then consider if you are spiritually dead. When God's Spirit is working inside of us, we will see the fruit. When we operate from the flesh, we see death and destruction. These two are at war, and whichever one you feed the most will win. You want the life that only the Spirit of God can produce, and you must intentionally sow to the Spirit.

The good news is that if you have gotten off track, God can restore you. First, you will need to repent. When we are under the influence of another spirit, we do not see the need to repent until we crash or fall because of pride. Then suddenly, we need God to rescue us, so we are more likely to repent at that time because we need Him.

Have you ever seen yourself sinking deeper and deeper, but you do not know how to stop? This is usually when sin has set in, and what started as a decision feels less of a decision and more of an addiction or a burden. The situation has spiraled out of control. Still, pray because God will restore you if you have faith. No matter what it looks like at this time, keep the faith. God works miracles. We believe and pray intentionally because we know when giving our burdens or issues to God with a sincere heart, He goes to work in our situation on our behalf.

That is how He manifests His glory in our lives. He does what we cannot do on our own. The bottom line, if you focus on pleasing your flesh, you will die, but if you focus on God and pleasing God, you will see miracles. God is always working miracles, and we need His grace. To truly see the fullness of God, we need to be obedient and operate according to His word. Sin only attempts to distract us from what God truly has for us.

## Serve Others

"5 Let this mind be in you, which was also in Christ Jesus: 6 Who, being in the form of God, thought it not robbery to be equal with God: 7 But made himself of no reputation, and took upon him the form of a servant, and was made in the likeness of men: 8 And being found in fashion as a man, he humbled himself, and became obedient unto death, even the death of the cross. 9 Wherefore God also hath highly exalted him and given him a name which is above every name: 10 That at the name of Jesus every knee should bow, of things in heaven, and things in earth, and things under the earth; 11 And that every tongue should confess that Jesus Christ is Lord, to the glory of God the Father." (Philippians 2:5-11 King James Version)

Often, we forget the responsibility that comes with the blessing. We are blessed to be a blessing. This is how we are purposeful in being fruitful and multiplying. When you become a conduit of blessings and serve others, God multiplies the blessing for us even more and through us. The key to genuine service is humility, and the key to humility is service. Serve, serve, and serve! "If serving is beneath you, leadership is above you!"

Humility does not mean that we do not have anything or that we are nothing but, rather, we know who we are and the purpose and God's intent for our lives. Our father in heaven supplies all our needs. It isn't a place of lack, considering the earth is the Lords and the fullness thereof. When we have the mind of Christ, we become more intentional, as was Christ, and His story does not end on a tree. He rose! He is seated at the right hand of God and has all power in His hands. "Looking unto Jesus the author and finisher of our faith; who for the joy that was set before him endured the cross, despising the shame, and is set down at the right hand of the throne of God." (Hebrews 12:2

Real success is not in what we do for ourselves but in what we do for others. Have you ever succeeded at something and celebrated by yourself? It can be lonely. Let us be honest. We end up finding someone to share our happiness with. Why? Because God did not intend for us to be alone. Be intentional in sharing your gifts and blessings with others. The more we care and share, the more God gives us because he can trust us to do His will on the earth.

Whether it is your church, community, family, or stranger, you will find a way to share your success with someone. Hopefully, it will not be with the wrong people or person but also be careful not to isolate yourself. Watch the company you keep and keep in mind God did not intend for you to be alone. Be intentional about the people you surround yourself with because the wrong company can bring many troubles. We shouldn't get so desperate that we find ourselves dancing with the devil. I know because I have been there. Sometimes we don't even realize it because they appear to be sheep when indeed they are wolves in sheep clothing.

Now I do not say this to look down on people who are not

where you are spiritually. Likewise, you should not participate in ungodly behaviors just for the company. We must raise the standard on that part. You can help others in many ways but make sure it is something God approves of and not your mission to fulfill a void in your own life. Many times, we can be lead down the wrong path just from having the wrong intentions. It is even possible to be lead down the wrong path with the right intentions. Therefore, we have to be discerning when it comes to the people we allow in our lives and their intentions.

Acts of service are the most significant indication of maturity in any area. When you no longer must hoard something for yourself, you become more generous. Generosity produces blessings from God. When we do the work in the land, God blesses us in spectacular ways. The harvest is plentiful, but the laborers are few. There are many people whose lives we can reach and touch, but we must be willing and generous. Let's sow some seeds of God's love and blessings throughout the land.

Don't be like some people. They count their blessings and attempt to keep them for themselves. Without understanding the principle of giving, most people will do this, especially if you grew up with a poverty mindset. Some people will try to ignore people who need help. Instead of wanting to help others, they become upset, bitter, and selfish. Do not be like them. God gives you blessings to be a blessing to others. This goes for your time, talents, and treasures.

God calls for us to be good stewards, and this is his will

for His people. That means it is directly related to your purpose, calling, and destiny. It could very much so be the missing piece of the puzzle. If this is you, I challenge you to give a generous donation to your church or a foundation that you know will do good by it, volunteer your time and services, and share your talents without expecting anything in return except God's blessing.

# Perseverance, Faithfulness, and Consistency

Do you ever get so excited about doing something you have always wanted to do, and then here comes Satan and his dwarfs to try to steal it? In this chapter, I want you to take your power back. God did not make any weak soldiers. He made soldiers who depend on and trust in Him, but we succeed because our strengths and abilities are limited. God is unlimited and can renew our strength and give us the wisdom to overcome any obstacle. We just have to believe.

Perseverance is one of the most critical strategies in success. You can bet that if you try to do anything significant, there will be opposition. Life happens, but the real jewel here is not just in being a victim to life's circumstances but in how we respond. This is the only part we are responsible for, our response. Let us break down that word *response-able*. Not only am I able to respond, but I can react in the best way possible when I take back my power to be responsible for my response and not to focus on other people's actions or things that are out of my control. When it is out of my control, I know that it is an opportunity for God to step in. In that case, my response is prayer. I still respond in love and according to God's word but let me be completely honest. I miss it sometimes too.

Have you ever watched a basketball game and the player shoots the ball and misses? It seems like it is going to go in, but no, he misses it. That is how it is in life. Sometimes we miss the mark, after which we can choose to ignore it and let that be the end but not in basketball. Both teams will be there looking for the rebound because that is where the real power is at that moment. We are over the fact that we missed it, but can we get the ball back and make the shot. You see, it is all in your response, and sometimes in life, it is just as quick as the basketball game. You must be ready to get the ball back and take the next shot.

Everyone has been in a situation where their patience was tried, and you still had to respond. You had to be responseable. At that very moment, everything you have done in practice will show. If you have been reading the word, if you have been praying, if you have been fasting, it will show if you have been intimate with God. If you have not been doing well in practice, it will show up in the game. Some of us do not even show up to practice, but we expect to succeed and win. Nobody is perfect, but the more we spend time with God, the more He endows us with His presence, full of power, wisdom, and glory. That is why I say we need to read and study the word but also fast and pray. It is in our intimacy with God that He prepares us for victory after victory.

There is only so far raw talent can take you. You must practice being prepared for those moments when you must respond. The basketball game is not only about offense where you have the ball and can make the shot, but it is equally defense where you will have to know how to respond. There are some things that no amount of practice can prepare you for but even with that, still trust God.

Pray, and God will fight your battles for you. God is available for us when we need Him. He promises never to leave us or forsake us, so in the most challenging situations, put your trust in God and not only in your strength or abilities. God can do what we are incapable of. We call it impossible because it is impossible for man, but it is not impossible for God.

Now there will be times when you just want to quit and throw in the towel. Do not. You must persevere. There is no real success where there are no challenges. Life all by itself will present challenges. There is no testimony without a test and no message without experiencing a mess. All things are working for our good when we are living a life of purpose in God. "28 And we know that all things work together for good to them that love God, to them who are the called according to his purpose." (Romans 8:28 King James Version)

We are in spiritual warfare, so naturally, there will be challenges. Battles are a part of the war. One of Satan's biggest goals is to try to get you to worship him, not God. He wants glory. He will go at any length to try to distract you and take your focus off God. If we focus so much on the problem, the problem will get bigger. If we focus on God, then we will see the salvation of the Lord in all our battles. God is mighty in action, and He has not lost one battle yet. Therefore, I say, take back your power. Do not just sit around and let the enemy beat up on you. You have weapons. Prayer is a weapon. The word is a weapon. Faith is a weapon. Praise is a weapon.

Now I know this can sound a bit much and that you know you will get tired sometimes. That is all right. God said, "Come to me, all you who are weary and burdened, and I will give you rest." (Matthew 11:28 New International Version) Even God made time for rest. Do not work yourself to death. Take time and rest. Later in this book, we are going to talk about healthy and balanced lifestyles. This is important because the disease is just that. It is when our bodies are not at ease (dis-ease).

We often wonder why we cannot fight off the cold or why we are suffering from depression. It is because we need to change. This does not mean give up on your goals. It is the opposite. It may just mean that you need balance or rest. Go to God when you are weak and watch him work on your behalf. A lack of rest is sometimes how the enemy will catch you off guard and attack harder when you have the least energy to fight. Please rest, mentally, spiritually, and physically but just do not quit. You must persevere. Sometimes there is no way around it, but you must go through it.

## PERSEVERE

**P**ush- you must push your way through.

**E**nergy- you will need power, so rest and keep a healthy lifestyle.

**R**esponsible- you need to respond to situations maturely andappropriately.

**S**urvive- you will have to fight your way through. That is why weput on the whole armor of God.

**E**agerly- go after your purpose eagerly with excitement andanticipation.

**V**ictory- we have the victory in Jesus. Remember, no matter what happens in battle, it is a fixed war, and we know the result in the end. We win.

**E**ffective- be effective at whatever you do. If it is not working, try other options. Just do not give up. Also, do not give up on something before it works.

**R**eflect- be honest with yourself. Consider where you are and where you are going.

**E**nthusiastic- stay hopeful and optimistic. Do not let that devil steal your joy!!!

Persevere!!! Persevere!!! Persevere!!!

## Faithfulness and Consistency

So, you have a little success, and here is where so many people miss it. They are so impressed by one little success that they forget that they must continue to stay in the game. One point is not going to make you entirely successful. Winning requires consistency. It is like perseverance but a little different. Have you ever been to the gym and got excited because you did your first workout towards the body you want? Then the next day comes, and something gets in the way. You lose momentum, and suddenly, months have gone by since you last went to the gym. You find yourself nowhere near your body goals or fitness goals. You have a problem with being consistent in that area. You will need to persist, yes, but equally, you have to know that you will have to do it consistently to get results. This is how it becomes a lifestyle change and not just a one-time act.

Real success is not overnight. It will be many days and many nights that lead to a lifestyle of success. You cannot just do one thing, and then that is it. It would help if you kept at it consistently. It takes faithfulness. Be always present for your success.

There was nothing wrong with the workout you did the first time. You just did not continue—you lost momentum. You did not persevere, so you do not get results. You want results. Try being consistent. It takes a level of discipline that stretches beyond your comfort zone. If you always do what you always did, you will always get the results you always had.

You will have to do it even when you do not want to, or it is not convenient. Set a goal and do it repeatedly. That is consistency. Now let us start with a small plan for practice. It can be ten minutes of working out a day or drinking eight glasses of water a day, but it just needs to be small to practice consistency. Keep track of your results. Choose whatever time is most convenient and then do it. Your follow-through is the most crucial aspect of your success.

Increase your goals as you conquer each one. If you go two weeks doing ten minutes of exercise every day, then take it up a notch and do twenty minutes a day. One thing is for sure, if you do not do anything, you will never get there, and you will not get there just doing it one time. Real success takes consistency, intentionality, strategy, steps, and action.

You want to fulfill your purpose in God. Do not just read the Bible one time and be done. Read it every day, and you will begin to see how God's word changes your life. You cannot expect results if you have not put in the work. God wants you to be successful. When we are successful in the kingdom, we bring Him glory.

Whether it is reading God's word, exercising, making an album, or writing a book, whatever it is, start today. Make small goals, be consistent in reaching your small goals, and eventually, reach for the much bigger goals. It is ok to start small but do start. If you have already started, it may be time to reach that next level.

Regarding competition, get rid of the idea altogether except when it is understood, of course, such as with sports. Just as one person's definition of success may be different from another is, in the same way, another person's win may be different as well. That is why the real competition is not with another individual but with yourself. We all should continuously improve in some way or some area of life.

Someone else's ruler does not measure your growth or success. I have heard people put it like this: do not compare your Chapter 1 with someone else's Chapter 20. You do not know what they had to go through to get where they are. Just focus on your growth. We should always have mentors, coaches, and leaders who are ahead of us. We can learn so much from other people's experiences but do not allow it to fool you into thinking it is easy. Like you have a journey and process, they have one too.

To win in life, you must know that the real battle is never with other people but with your current mindset. Do you want to see real change and growth? Here is the key. You must change the way you think. It is your present mindset you have grown accustomed to that may be the problem. It will require a paradigm shift. You must challenge your limiting beliefs and push past them if they are not serving your purpose.

You must change the way you think before you can truly change your results. Even though studying God's word to renew your mind and obeying the word is necessary, you can change your mindset, but it will require a change in your behavior or actions to see results in your life. Step outside of your comfort zone. Try something you have never done before. For me, it was going live on social media. I had done it before, but I wanted to step out of my comfort zone, so I challenged myself to show up more. The first time I was so nervous, I spoke so fast out of fear and excitement, but as soon as I started getting back feedback from those who were there or watched the replay, I was overwhelmed by the positive feedback. Comfort zones only leave us stuck right where we are. You cannot be upset for not having the results for work you did not do.

Humble beginnings do not always look like success, but they indeed are. For most people, just getting started is a huge battle. They have the vision, but they cannot seem to build up the momentum to get started, or, if you are like I was, you have every excuse in the book. It is only when you get tired of feeling sorry for yourself and get the courage to at least try that you can even start. So, starting is an accomplishment. However, once you get started, you will look around and see people turning cartwheels around you, and suddenly, you want to quit. Let other people's success motivate you and not intimidate you. Just think of it this way, if they could succeed at it, then so can you. And if you keep a positive attitude, you may learn a thing or two. Humility comes before honor.

Remember, your biggest competition is your current mindset because it is comfortable, and it is not other people. You cannot be great and lazy, too. You cannot be powerful and pitiful. You must show up as your best version of who you are today and show yourself some grace. It is all about progression, not perfection. Progress is measurable. Perfection is relative.

Even if all you have is potential, let that speak for you. You will build confidence along the way. I believe I can do all things through Christ. So, whether I am a beginner at something or an expert, I believe in excellence. God can do what I cannot, so my trust is in God, but I do my best. I am not vulnerable or insecure because I know that greater is He in me than He in the world. Now do not get it twisted. I do have fears, but the real victory is in conquering those fears with faith.

If you want to build your confidence, try facing your fears. Push past the fear and be courageous. It will show you that there is more in you than you ever knew existed. Now, this does not mean you should be swimming with sharks unless that is your thing. I am just telling you to pick something small and face it and learn something about yourself. Same with God. Pray about it, put it in God's hands, and trust Him with it, and watch what happens next. Even a tiny step is a step. It is in those small steps that we build the courage for the much more significant battles.

One of my fears was public speaking until I did it. Now I get on stage and share my testimony, my talents, and more. All because I faced the fear. I was not great at first, but I got better and better each time. That is usually how it works. You start. You do your best. You fail and succeed to some degree. That is fine because now you know your strengths and weaknesses. You can use that to set next-level goals. What is a next-level goal? A next-level goal is precisely that. A goal that will propel you forward to your next level. Whatever that may look like for you. It is all about forward motion.

God is our real audience, but we are no good if we cannot serve others or let our work glorify God. So be intentional about the amount of effort you put into being successful. Be great because you are great. God made you great because we were made in His image, and He is excellent. We can all do so much more than we are doing at this present time, but we have to stretch our faith a little, persevere through challenges, be consistent and be willing to contribute to society and the kingdom. Being a servant often motivates me to push past my own convictions and comfort zones. When thinking of helping others, I want to go a little bit further and do a little more. God honors this. "13 Greater love hath no man than this, that a man lay down his life for his friends." (John 15:13 King James Version)

## GETTING RESULTS AND SEEING MANIFESTATION

In 2019, I embarked on a journey of purpose. I knew that it would require faith. I knew that although God had given me the instructions and the vision, nothing - and I mean nothing - was going to happen unless I did my part.

I recall quitting my job and becoming a stay-at-home mom and using that time to be productive and write my first book, *Priceless*. It felt quite like being in a cocoon. I was alone for a reason. Of course, I had my newborn and my other children, but I did not have a typical day out of my home with large groups of people on a job. You would think I would have gotten lonely because usually, in the past, I did, but God never left me lonely. I was happy, fulfilled, and working within my purpose.

When God said, now's the time to write the book that He placed in my heart, I immediately started planning. I could not wait to share my testimony. One vision and victory lead to another and then lead to another. Pretty soon, I saw the manifestation of a total transformation in my spirituality.

I became a published author and then a coach. I had big plans, but God's plans were even bigger. God planned to use the gifts and my testimony as I also became a minister of the Gospel. Proverbs 19:21 says, "Many are the plans in a man's heart, but it is the LORD's purpose thatprevails."

So, when I speak of manifestations, I am not talking about vain pursuits of exploiting God's true power. I am talking about when you know that you know what you have been called to do. Your conviction to do it is more robust than your complacency or excuses. If God said it, then that settles it. This does not eradicate our responsibility of obeying God and doing our part.

1 Corinthians 3:6 says, "One man soweth, another man watereth, but only God can give the increase." One of the key things I like about this scripture is that it gives Paul credit for planting the seed. It also gives recognition to Apollos for watering the seed. Still, there is even more glory to God for the manifestation. Just imagine planting the seed and watering it every day, never to see the fruit. It would seem to be a waste of time, but it is not. It requires faith in God to give the increase.

I remember writing my book "Priceless" and thinking who is going to buy this. Then I started getting so many responses from family members and friends that I felt completely supported. This is not to mention the signs and wonders I was getting from God. I knew God completely supported me. Sometimes we don't see how it is possible, but if we just obey God, we will see Him hasten to perform His word. I have truly seen God take that book and pivot me into my destiny. I don't worry about sales. I am more concerned with souls. I have been so blessed. My finances are blessed, my family is blessed, my ministry is blessed. I am truly blessed to be a blessing.

Speaking of plants, we know that a plant starts as a seed. When God created everything, He made it so that every plant would produce seeds and those seeds would produce more seeds. There is always a bigger picture. He made it so that each part of His creation would continue to procreate and be fruitful and multiply. That is God's will for His creation.

While we have certainly evolved, God's basic principle of seed, time, and harvest is set in stone for eternity. Fruition is the state in which the seed that was planted produces the fruit of its kind. It is not a new topic or discussion, but we have a hard time seeing how it relates to our own lives, but the answer is right there in Genesis.

Everything on Earth is a seed in some way. Even nonliving things such as metal and stones because are used to create other objects even though they do not reproduce in the same sense. In that case, it is the seed of future creations.

God wants us, His creation, to create and reproduce. In other words, He wants us to be fruitful and multiply and have dominion over the Earth. We were made in the image of God, so, like our Heavenly Father, we are creators. Our spiritual gifts are also seeding. They are seeds planted inside of us to fulfill His purpose on Earth. Not only for our own sake but for others and for future generations to come. The book I wrote, "Priceless," was definitely therapeutic for me but when I think of my children and my children's children reading my story, I get even more overwhelmed with joy.

Acts of faith are not just actions that we take, hoping and wishing that something will happen. It is what we do in faith, knowing that God will give the increase. An idea is a seed. A vision is a seed that God planted inside of us. Our actions should be intentional and lead to producing the type of fruit we are asking God for, but no amount of effort will change the fact that true increase comes from God. God goes beyond the surface and produces victories that are not just ours to keep for ourselves but that will serve others as well.

When we realize God is the only one who can give us an increase, it puts us in a state of humility as well. We recognize that we cannot do anything without God, but all things are possible with God. What good is planting the seed and watering it if it cannot produce a good harvest? Knowing only God can increase helps us rest assured that if God called you to do it, then He's going to provide the provision and the increase at the proper time.

When we focus on what we want without having any meaningfulness behind it, it is vain. "But seek ye first the kingdom of God and His righteousness, and all these things shall be added unto you." (Matthew 6:33 King James Version) God wants us to live Godly lives obeying His word seeking Him, not just things. That is why so many of us get this whole manifestation thing misconstrued. One of the biggest misconceptions that we have regarding manifestation is that it is evil and witchcraft. That is mainly because the world has taken the concept and made it sound like it is just this cheap way of getting whatever you want. As if God is our genie, and we go around ordering Him around. It is interesting because that would explain why it fails so many people. Manifestation in the kingdom of God is so much greater than that. So instead of us ordering Him around, He orders our steps.

Just think about a garden. That is precisely where we started and where He gave us His first instructions for mankind in the first place. Adam and Eve were in the garden when God told them to be fruitful and multiply. It is beyond having a family, although that is part of it. A garden is an environment of growth and abundance. It is God's will for our lives but where we go wrong often is that our desire is more for earthly possessions and distractions than they are for the things of God and His principles and standards.

You can have as many material things as you want and still be unsatisfied and unfulfilled because they are empty without meaningfulness and love. Mark 8:36 (King James Version) says, "For what shall it profit a man, if he shall gain the whole world, and lose his own soul?" So, with that in mind, just having things is not a true manifestation. It could even be a distraction from the real thing, like a weed instead of wheat. One is suitable for food, and the other is trash, just like the parable in Matthew 13.

John 15:16 (King James Version) says, "Ye have not

chosen me, but I have chosen you, and ordained you, that ye should go and bring forth fruit, and that your fruit should remain: that whatsoever ye shall ask of the Father in my name, he may give it to you." That is why we can believe Him for the increase. If God said we could have it, then that settles it. We go wrong when we start thinking these things are more important than seeking the kingdom of God. That is why it is an illusion. It is in the kingdom of God that we find fulfillment, peace, joy, andlove.

So, seek ye first the kingdom of God, and let us keep first things first related to a believer's life. God never said that we could not have the desires of our hearts. He is just making sure we do not make idols of things and forget our existence's true purpose. God is a jealous God, and He does not want anything before Him. When we are intimate with God, we become one with God. That means we want what God wants for us, and He wants to give us the desires of our hearts when, of course, they are lined up with His will (His Word).

Just imagine everything God says you can have in His word; you can have. After you see it in your mind, write the vision and make it plain. Then, speak it into existence and allow God's word to take root in your heart. If you honestly believe, you will have actions that demonstrate your belief in God. No actions, no faith. No faith, no results.

Many people believe so much in their works and stand by their results. Some find it hard to believe in God and what God can do, as far as miracles, breakthroughs, and manifestations. Their abilities and experiences are limited to only what they can accomplish in their power and strength. They have denied the supernatural power of God, and so they forfeit the power that comes with it. The Bible says, "Those who think carnally cannot understand spiritual things because they are foolish to the carnal way of thinking." (1 Corinthians 2:14)

So, regarding manifestation and worldly views, one thing that has been popular in this last decade or so has been the law of attraction. Many people have started hoping and wishing it would be their path to happiness. Even though some of it is like biblical principles, it is not the same thing. John 2:24 (King James Version) says, "They that worship him must worship him in spirit and truth." We are not just talking about this gravitational field that only functions based on our vibrating frequencies but rather in trusting God and being led by His Spirit. One causes stress and anxiety about always getting it right and our own human power, but the other is about surrendering to God and His power.

I have even found that God has stepped in and worked miracles for me at some of my lowest times. Not when I was vibrating high, but when the only thing I had left was faith in God. I said a prayer, and God answered my prayer. That is what faith in God can do.

Manifestation is not based on just our works, although we do have a part to play in executing the vision God gave us. It is indeed based on our faith in God, and if we say we believe in God and we genuinely do, then our actions will line up with what we say we believe, in some shape, form, or fashion.

"Faith without works is dead." (James 2:26 New King James Version) Bottom line, you cannot say you believe God for an increase, a victory, or any change for that matter if you are not doing anything yourself to get the results.

James 2:18 (King James Version) says, "18 Yea, a man may say, Thou hast faith, and I have works: shew me thy faith without thy works, and I will shew thee my faith by my works."

Faith is what you do as a result of what you believe. As in the previous example, when you sit in a chair, you do not overthink it. If the chair looks like a standard chair, you probably will sit down because you believe that the chair will hold you up. You cannot have true faith without it being demonstrated by your actions. You do what you do because of what you believe. If you are not seeing results or manifestation of God's visions, do not blame God but take a deeper look at yourself and your beliefs. Are they lining up with God's will for your life, or are they guided by the enemy's tactics and lies?

## Rest and Restore

On this journey of faith and purpose, it is essential to be well-balanced. As you grow through the journey, there will be all sorts of challenges, tests, and trials. You will experience stretching and, in some cases, straight-up spiritual warfare. You will have to stay prayed up and study the word every day. It will require your focus on God, and sometimes it will be like stepping out of the fiery furnace with no smoke or ashes. Like, how did I make it through that? Nobody but God!

Sometimes we see other people's lives and think they got there overnight. The truth is everyone has a process, and it is not always easy. After you have spent time growing the vision God gave you, must take time to rest and be restored. God is not through with you. You may have completed an assignment or project, but you are not done.

Sometimes God just wants us to take a moment and relax. You worked hard. You have thought to yourself, this is good, and now just like our Heavenly Father, it is time to rest. When we rest, we get restored and re-energized to go to the next set of instructions, the following vision, and the next level in fulfilling our purpose here on Earth. As long as you are alive, there is purpose to fulfill.

When we have done our part, we can rest in God's promises that He will give the increase. We can be content with what we have accomplished but ultimately, we prepare for the next chapter. You cannot pour from an empty cup.

When we do not rest, we find ourselves burned out and of no good use to the kingdom. We must learn to do all that we can do and trust God. Looking back at creation, God spoke most everything into existence, and then He created and formed mankind with His hands. Yep. We are that significant to Him that He got His hands in the dirt and shaped and molded us. Then He took His breath and breathed the breath of life into our lungs. On the 7th day, when He was done, He rested. He called that day the Sabbath and called that day Holy. By law, some rules and laws had to be followed to keep the Sabbath Holy. Mankind was not to work on this day but rather use this day to revere God and creation. God did not rest because He was tired or sleepy. He rested because He knew we would need to know that there is a time to work and a time to rest. He laid the foundation for us to follow. We are made in His image, right? So, what does that mean for us?

Now there is also such a thing as balance in life. We cannot be all go and no rest. We would crash. We need to have a healthy and balanced life. Our bodies are the temples of the Holy Spirit, and so we do need to take care of them to fulfill the purpose God has for our lives.

What is a healthy balanced lifestyle? Let us look back at

creation. God created the Earth in six days and rested one. We can learn a lot about God in this context. He spoke this world into existence. He formed humankind and breathed life into our mortal bodies. He gave instructions, and He rested. There is so much to say about that. God rested. If God rested, then you know we need rest.

Also, God created full days. He created days for us to work and evenings for us to rest. When we rest, we regain the energy to face another purposeful day. We have work to do, but we are less productive when we do not rest. Your body will likely shut down on you. If it does not shut down, you will not be your complete self and produce your best conscious work. We all must take time to rest to be restored.

Have you ever done reps of an exercise? In between reps, you would rest. Why? Your body needs to reset its energy to receive the total capacity of the workout. So, you rest in between, and then you do it again. There are long rests and short rests. Do you have a Monday through Friday job, but by Wednesday, you are ready for the weekend because you are looking forward to resting? During the day, most of us take our first 15-minute break within the first couple of hours of work. Then let's not forget the almighty lunch break.

Let's face it; we need to rest. It is even mandatory by law.

We need a lot more than just working towards our goals and making accomplishments. A healthy, balanced lifestyle requires rest. Yes, set your fitness goals. Write your business goals. Set your family goals. Set your time with God, keeping in mind God is always with us but more so for study and prayer. Set your ministry goals. Set your goals because if you fail to plan, you plan to fail, but after you have done all of that, make sure you take time to rest.

Rest is not just sleeping. Rest is a pause, a break, a moment to regain momentum and stamina. Be great but rest, which is another aspect of God's fullness, peace, and abundance. He says, "Come to me, all you who are weary and burdened, and I will give you rest." (Matthew 11:28 New International Version) This is also evidence that God wants us to have rest. But what is this rest that He is referring to? This rest is a state of mind, body, and spirit. The rest He is referring to is peace. If you ever get to the point when you cannot go anymore or take any more, go to God, and He will give you rest. Do not wait until you are stressed out. Go to God for rest throughout the day, and He will balance the ups and downs of life. He is the source of happiness, health, wealth, and wholeness.

We are complete in Him. God wants us to be whole and find everything we need in Him. It is contentment. Contentment does not mean being so satisfied that I stopped pressing or stopped pursuing God and His purpose for my life. Contentment is a state of fulfillment, happiness, wholeness, and satisfaction in God.

Concentrate on these scriptures and make it a daily confession. This will remind you that it is God's will that we are happy, healthy, wealthy, and whole.

"Dear friend, I pray that you are prospering in every way and are in good health, just as your whole life is going well." (3 John 1:2 Christian Standard Bible)

"The thief comes only to steal and kill and destroy; I have come that they may have life and have it to the full." (John 10:10 New International Version)

"For I know the plans I have for you," declares the LORD, "plans to prosper you and not to harm you, plans to give you hope and a future." (Jeremiah 29:11 New International Version) If God gave you the plan, we could rest assured that He will provide the provision and the increase. It is time out for putting off for tomorrow what you can do today. Do not be the one, when the master returns, who has buried their talent. Do your part and work. Do your part and rest.

Rest in the faithful and never-failing arms of God. God is faithful. God never fails. He will raise us at that right time. Do what you are supposed to do and trust God for the increase. When you trust God, you can sleep better because you know that your trust is not misplaced. It is in God's hands.

## Conclusion

So, here is the conclusion of the matter. You have everything you need right there inside of you. Draw it out like deep waters. Life changes when you honestly believe God is living inside of you.

There is a difference because we do not live from the

outside. We live from the inside out. No matter what you take in from the outside, ultimately, it is what is in you that is going to come out. Does it matter what you put in you? Absolutely. What you put in is what will come out, but here is how it all starts - from the inside. It is your decision.

You decide what to read, eat, do, and pursue. You, yes, you. Sure, there are things and circumstances that you will have to endure in this life. No one said it was easy, but it is worth it. Your spiritual relationship with God on this journey is the most important thing because this life is spiritual. You will not get anywhere just looking at your circumstances and seeing things from a carnal standpoint. If you want to see a true manifestation of God in every part of your life, you are going to have to give Him every part of you. As He leads and guides you on this path, stay focused on Him, keep the faith, and be bold and courageous because you have God the Almighty working everything out for your good.

So, what are you afraid of? Pursuing your goals? Fear is not an option. Although it does come up, we have power over it. To live your best life, you need courage. It would not take courage if it were going to be easy. God told Joshua to be bold and very courageous. (Joshua 1:9) Do it with God leading and guiding you. Do it, afraid. Do it in faith. This is your best chance of success. It is the only real success, being in the will of God. If God is for you, who can be against you?

Now for some people, it is not the fear of pursuing purpose but rather the fear of inadequacy. Am I good enough? Yes, with God, you are more than enough. Romans 8:37 says,

"We are more than conquerors through him who loves us." Even still, there is always room for growth and maturity in any area of our lives. Paul said in Philippians 3:12-14 (King James Version), "12 Not as though I had already attained, either were already perfect: but I follow after, if that I may apprehend that for which also, I am apprehended of Christ Jesus. 13Brethren, I count not myself to have apprehended: but this one thing I do, forgetting those things which are behind, and reaching forth unto those things which are before, 14 I press toward the mark for the prize of the high calling of God in Christ Jesus."

While you continue to grow in faith and your predestined purpose, remember, you will not get anywhere without starting. Skill is cultivated and developed over time. Talent is a natural God-given gift, but it takes skill to perfect your talents. You should take your natural talents and nurture them with impeccable skills. You should take your passion, that thing that God has placed deep in your heart, and create visions. Pray about it and ask God. He will reveal it to you, and if it is not so big that you don't need Him, that's not it. God does miracles. Remember that, and don't be afraid to trust Him.

A lot of us have this fear of flying. It is a fear that if I begin to soar, I could fall. It is a fear of heights. Do not you know God is with you everywhere you go, and you are not perfect now, and you will not be then. Not until we are in our glorified bodies and no longer in the flesh. Now that is not an excuse to stay stagnant or stay where you are. Just because the flesh calls do not mean you have to answer.

When the Spirit of God calls, the key is to answer that call asap and if you fall short, repent, but you certainly do not have to fear heights. God is with you now, and He will be with you then.

Have you ever met someone with fear or anxiety? If you have, or even if it is you, think about it along the same lines. You are safe, but you are panicking from a fear that is all inside your head. It is so real to you, but other people who do not have that fear see you sweat, and they think, why are you so afraid? Well, it is sort of like that. You are tripping while everyone else sees no real reason why you cannot soar. The reality is as it relates to anxiety. Illusions are real to the people who think them in their heads and believe them.

Therefore, the Bible says, "Cast down imaginations because your imagination could be the very thing holding back." The only way to overcome fear is to face it.

Now when I talk about flying, I am speaking metaphorically. Do not jump off a building to fly, of course. We know better than this because if you do, gravity will pull you down. You will not fly. You will, instead, fall. Use wisdom—moral of the story. We are not birds but metaphorically speaking, we can soar.

Isaiah 40:31 (New International Version)

"31 but those who hope in the LORD will renew their strength. They will soar on wings like eagles; they will run and not grow weary; they will walk and not be faint."

I do not want to speak of anxiety as an easy thing to deal with. We must have an intimate relationship with God to make it in this life. He also provides people in the form of doctors, therapists, and counselors to help you deal with these issues when it is not as simple as canceling out a thought. I have found what works for me is learning a new scripture every week and meditating on God's word. It reassures me that God is still in control and that I do not need to worry no matter what it looks like. It is a peace that surpasses all understanding. (Philippians 4:7)

Another thing that works for me is focusing on my blessings and not what I do not have. Gratitude is the attitude. A lot of people are pursuing, but not a lot of people are genuinely happy. The depression numbers are increasing every day. Every day new people are coming out about their depression and mental state. While this is very real, there are some situations where if you just talk to a person, it is as simple as learning coping skills. Once a few things do not go according to plan, they are suffering from depression. This is a trick of the enemy to try to get you to focus on what is wrong and what is lacking versus what is right and what you have. Count your blessings, not your issues. No matter what it is, God will get you through it even if you need help which we all do at some point on our journeys.

Gratitude is when we have an attitude of gratefulness. This does not mean you are settling for mediocrity. It just means while you are going through life's journey, you are not allowing the challenges and struggles to overcome you. Instead, you overcome them. This is how you find joy. When things happen that are hard to understand and cope with, we have the Holy Spirit, a comforter, and a guide. You can trust God to provide comfort in your time of need.

An attitude of gratitude is necessary as you embark on your journey with God because, remember, the real journey is spiritual. So, if you are negative, you will attract more negative situations spiritually. If you speak negatively, you will attract more negative situations. The power of life and death is in the tongue. (Proverbs 18:21)

Likewise, if you have an attitude of gratitude, that will bring you more gratitude, joy, and things to be grateful for. Whatever you focus on will grow if you are looking to pursue your purpose and calling, then the purpose will manifest. Part of growing is concentrating on that and not letting this world distract you.

Gratitude will also teach you patience. Patience is not how long you wait but your attitude while you wait. "And be not conformed to this world: but be ye transformed by the renewing of your mind, that ye may prove what that good is, and acceptable, and perfect, will of God." (Romans 12:2 King James Version)

Do not overwhelm your mind by chasing things. Instead, pursue God in every area of your life and His will. You are not just seeking goals. You want all that God has in store for you. It is a lifestyle.

Indeed, we should be pursuing God, and He will show us the way to the abundant, prosperous life He promised us in

His word.

Trust God in the process. Remember, mistakes are lessons and blessings in disguise. You learn and grow while pursuing God, your purpose, and your destiny in Him. Please do not give up no matter what and continue to act in faith because there is no faith in it. So, I leave you with these questions and a challenge. What will you do differently now that you have taken this journey with me by reading this book? What fear or challenge are you going to face with courage intentionally? What vision are you going to pursue that you have been putting off? In what ways will you seek God more for your purpose in Him?

## Here's the Challenge:

Pray and ask God for a vision.

Seek Him earnestly for your purpose.

As He begins to show you, write the vision.

Ask Him for instructions and speak as if it is already so. Take intentional actions in the right direction.

Remain persistent, faithful, and consistent. Do not give up no matter what.

Watch God manifest the vision in your life. Rest, Relax, Repeat!!!

Easier said than done? I know what you may be thinking

but trust me, faith works. Be all that God has called you to be and trust Him as He leads you on your journey. Pray, speak over your life in faith, be intentional and purposeful, persevere through the challenges, be consistent and trust God with the increase. You are enough. When God made you, He already knew what He had in mind for you, and it is all in His word. You do not have to settle another day for a lifeless than God's best. So, here is the challenge: write that vision that God gave you and make it plain. Then ask God for direction and as He shows you, write it down and trust and obey Him. Simply put, act in faith as per God's word, both written and spoken.

I hope this book has been a blessing to you and has encouraged you in some way. It would be irresponsible to share all this information to motivate you and get you hype about possibilities without mentioning that it requires discipline and obedience. There will be some changes that you will have to make to answer the call of God in your life. He will show you. You just have to trust Him and obey.

You may have to change your people, places, and things. If it is not in alignment with God's will for your life, then it must go.

Manifestation is spiritual. Even if you want to manifest something in the natural, it starts with the spiritual. An idea can be developed into a vision when we pray and ask God for the vision. He can show us many things through the supernatural if we just seek Him. We must pray and ask God what He wants us to do in and with our lives. Then allow Him to show us things that we never thought could happen for us, but all things are possible with God through Christ. That is the kind of God we serve. The God of miracles.

Do not doubt Him or His abilities to use you and bless you in your life. If you do your part and trust God for the increase, you will see the manifestation of the visions that He gave you. Hold on, and never give up. There is always a process, but you will reap a harvest in due season if you do not give up. Genesis 8:22 (KJV) says, "While the earth remaineth, seedtime and harvest, and cold and heat, and summer and winter, and day and night shall not cease."

The harvest is coming, but you have to believe, and when you don't, ask God to help you with your unbelief. He is faithful and just. There is nothing He won't do for those who love Him and are called according to His will.

# Be Encouraged

Hebrews 11 (New International Version)

Faith in Action

1 Now faith is confidence in what we hope for and assurance about what we do not see. 2 This is what the ancients were commended for.

3 By faith we understand that the universe was formed at God's command, so that what is seen was not made out of what was visible.

4 By faith Abel brought God a better offering than Cain did. By faith he was commended as righteous, when God spoke well of his offerings. And by faith Abel still speaks, even though he is dead.

5 By faith Enoch was taken from this life, so that he did not experience death: "He could not be found, because God had taken him away." For before he was taken, he was commended as one who pleased God. 6 And without faith it is impossible to please God, because anyone who comes to him must believe that he exists and that he rewards those who earnestly seek him.

7 By faith Noah, when warned about things not yet seen, in holy fear built an ark to save his family. By his faith he condemned the world and became heir of the righteousness that is in keeping with faith.

8 By faith Abraham, when called to go to a place he would later receive as his inheritance, obeyed and went, even though he did not know where he was going. 9 By faith he made his home in the promised land like a stranger in a foreign country; he lived in tents, as did Isaac and Jacob, who were heirs with him of the same promise. 10 For he was looking forward to the city with foundations, whose architect and builder is God. 11 And by faith even Sarah, who was past childbearing age, was enabled to bear children because she b considered him faithful who had made the promise. 12 And so from this one man, and he as good as dead, came descendants as numerous as the stars in the sky and as countless as the sand on the seashore.

13 All these people were still living by faith when they died. They did not receive the things promised; they only saw them and welcomed them from a distance, admitting that they were foreigners and strangers on earth. 14 People who say such things show that they are looking for a country of their own. 15 If they had been thinking of the country they had left, they would have had opportunity to return. 16 Instead, they were longing for a better country—a heavenly one. Therefore God is not ashamed to be called their God, for he has prepared a city for them.

17 By faith Abraham, when God tested him, offered Isaac as a sacrifice. He who had embraced the promises was about to sacrifice his one and only son, 18 even though God had said to him, "It is through Isaac that your offspring will be reckoned." 19 Abraham reasoned that God could even raise the dead, and so in a manner of speaking he did receive Isaac back from death.

20 By faith Isaac blessed Jacob and Esau in regard to their future.

21 By faith Jacob, when he was dying, blessed each of Joseph's sons, and worshiped as he leaned on the top of his staff.

22 By faith Joseph, when his end was near, spoke about the exodus of the Israelites from Egypt and gave instructions concerning the burial of his bones.

23 By faith Moses' parents hid him for three months after he was born, because they saw he was no ordinary child, and they were not afraid of the king's edict.

24 By faith Moses, when he had grown up, refused to be known as the son of Pharaoh's daughter. 25 He chose to be mistreated along with the people of God rather than to enjoy the fleeting pleasures of sin. 26 He regarded disgrace for the sake of Christ as of greater value than the treasures of Egypt,

because he was looking ahead to his reward. 27 By faith he left Egypt, not fearing the king's anger; he persevered because he saw him who is invisible. 28 By faith he kept the Passover and the application of blood, so that the destroyer of the firstborn would not touch the firstborn of Israel.

29 By faith the people passed through the Red Sea as on dry land; but when the Egyptians tried to do so, they were drowned.

30 By faith the walls of Jericho fell, after the army had marched around them for seven days.

31 By faith the prostitute Rahab, because she welcomed the spies, was not killed with those who were disobedient.

32 And what more shall I say? I do not have time to tell about Gideon, Barak, Samson and Jephthah, about David and Samuel and the prophets, 33 who through faith conquered kingdoms, administered justice, and gained what was promised; who shut the mouths of lions, 34 quenched the fury of the flames, and escaped the edge of the sword; whose weakness was turned to strength; and who became powerful in battle and routed foreign armies. 35 Women received back their dead, raised to life again. There were others who were tortured, refusing to be released so that they might gain an even better resurrection. 36 Some faced jeers and flogging, and even chains and imprisonment. 37 They were put to death by stoning; they were sawed in two; they were killed by the

sword. They went about in sheepskins and goatskins, destitute, persecuted and mistreated— 38 the world was not worthy of them. They wandered in deserts and mountains, living in caves and in holes in the ground.

39 These were all commended for their faith, yet none of them received what had been promised, 40 since God had planned something better for us so that only together with us would they be made perfect.

## AUTHOR PAGE

Shemeka Banks is a wife, mother of four, minister, coach, musician, and author. She has a Master's Degree in Christian Counseling, Bachelor's Degree in Law and Business, and an Associate's in Accounting. Her mission is to fight against the forces of depression, stress, low self-esteem, living aimlessly, and any evil spirit that seeks to destroy God's people. She is the author of the book "Priceless *7 Key Strategies to Spiritual Transformation*" and the "Priceless Devotional," both published in 2020. In 2015, she experienced a traumatic downfall that led her to a deep depression. She has since then discovered her purpose in life. She is the CEO of Misfitz Apparel and Purposed for Change. She is a recording artist that goes by the name SuperMeek. God restored her life after depression and is the super to her natural (SuperMeek). God afforded her the miraculous transformation that changed her life forever. She is now walking in her purpose and calling and encouraging others to do the same as well.

Made in the USA
Columbia, SC
06 April 2025